Miracles LIKE You AND Me

WRITTEN BY: **Rabbi Jason Bonder**
ILLUSTRATED BY: **Julie Wohl**

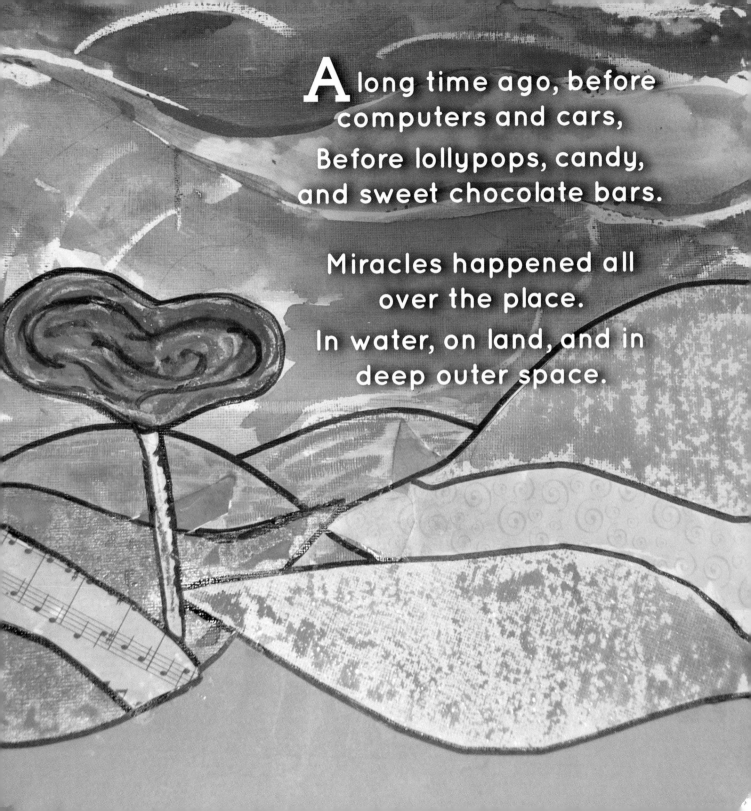

A long time ago, before computers and cars, Before lollypops, candy, and sweet chocolate bars.

Miracles happened all over the place. In water, on land, and in deep outer space.

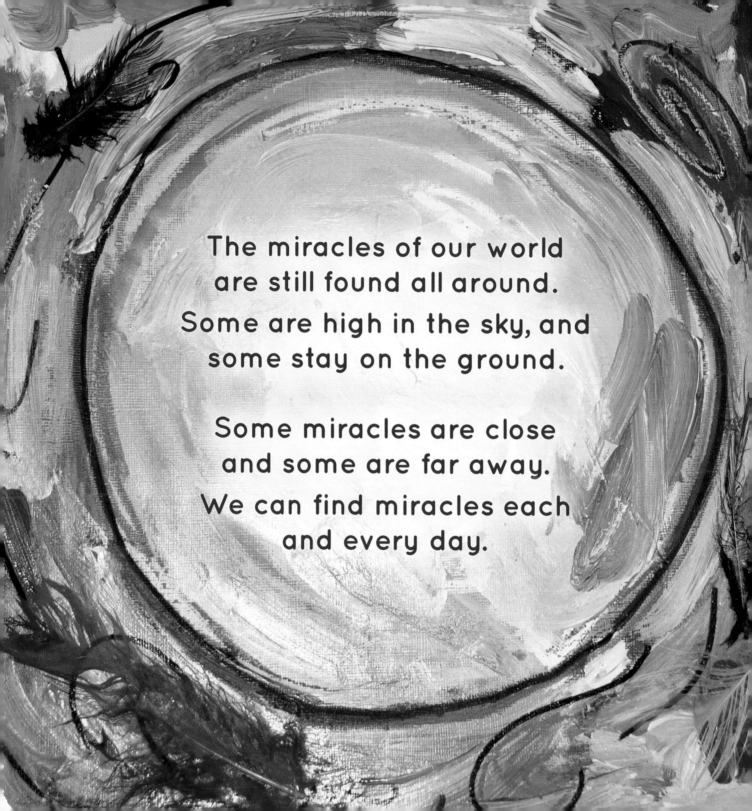

The miracles of our world
are still found all around.
Some are high in the sky, and
some stay on the ground.

Some miracles are close
and some are far away.
We can find miracles each
and every day.

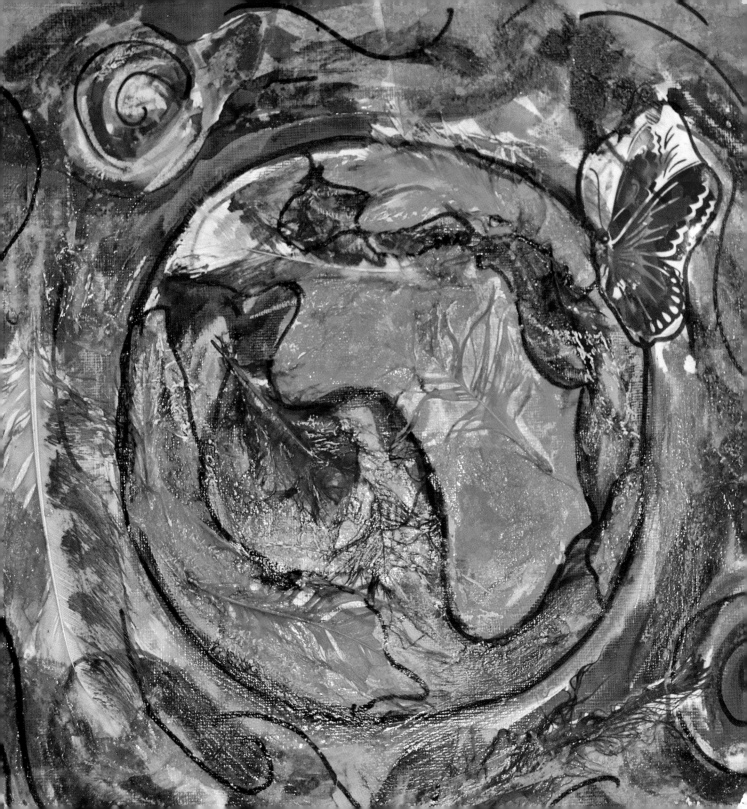

This first miracle wakes
us up from the night.
It keeps our earth warm,
and makes our days bright.

If we wake up real early
and look to the skies,
We can see this miracle,
and watch the sun rise!

In this miracle we can
splish and splash.
We can sit on the shore and
hear its waves crash

We can swim in this miracle.
It is in our reach,
Water is a miracle we
can find at the beach!

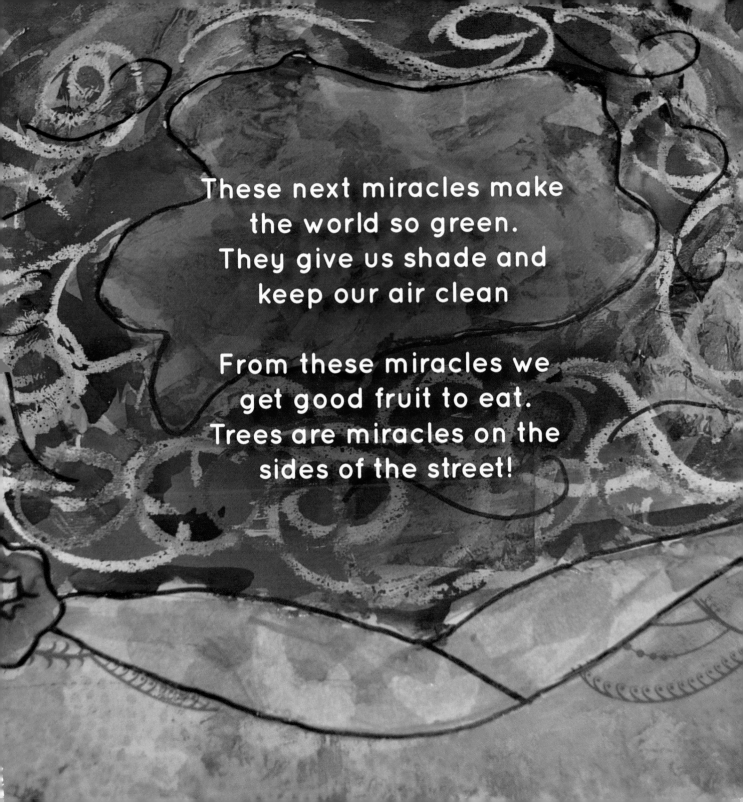

These next miracles make
the world so green.
They give us shade and
keep our air clean

From these miracles we
get good fruit to eat.
Trees are miracles on the
sides of the street!

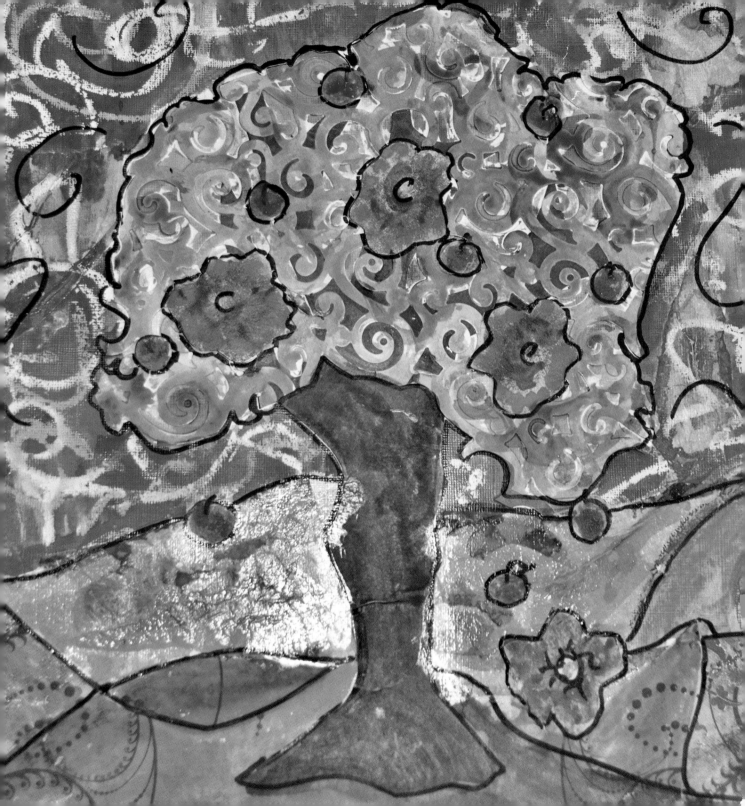

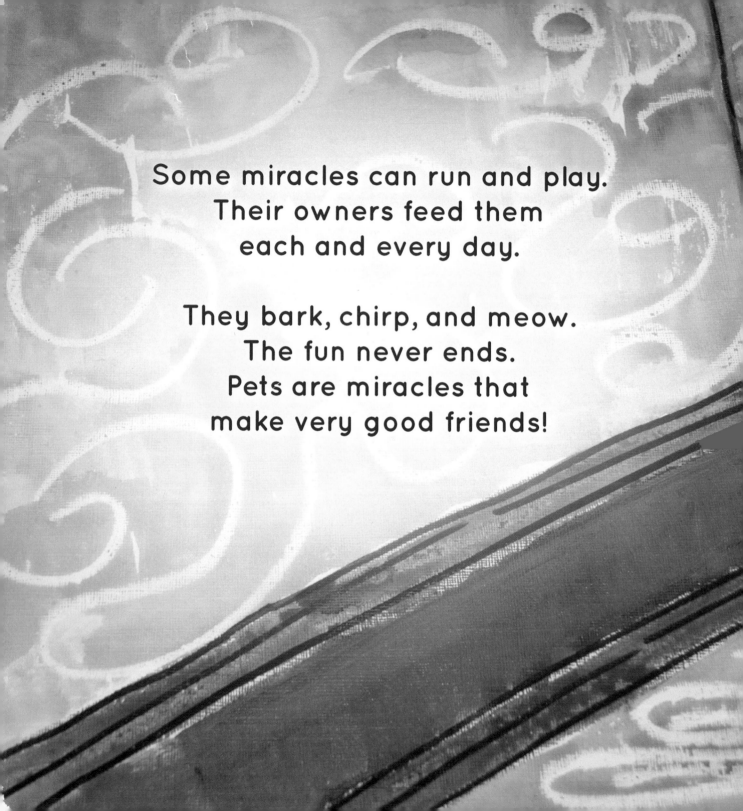

Some miracles can run and play.
Their owners feed them
each and every day.

They bark, chirp, and meow.
The fun never ends.
Pets are miracles that
make very good friends!

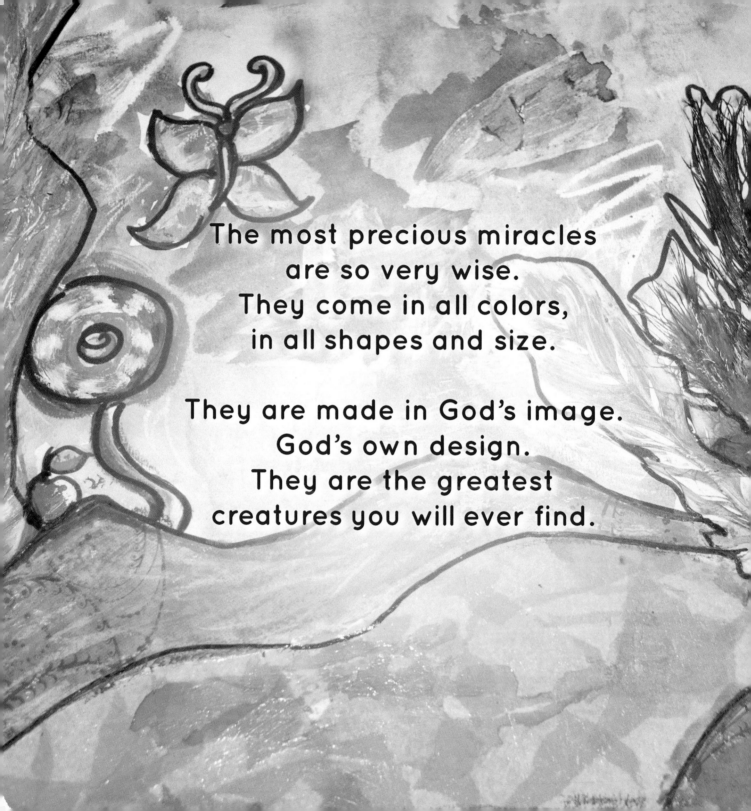

The most precious miracles
are so very wise.
They come in all colors,
in all shapes and size.

They are made in God's image.
God's own design.
They are the greatest
creatures you will ever find.

You can find these miracles under the sun.
They swim in the water and have lots of fun.

They like to relax under trees in the shade.
They enjoy all the miracles
that have been made.

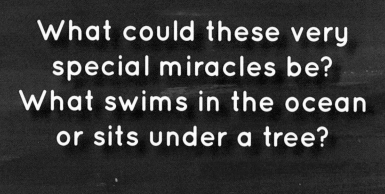

What could these very
special miracles be?
What swims in the ocean
or sits under a tree?

You can see one in the mirror.
It's so easy to see.

So always respect your
moms and dads. Cheer up
your friends when they are sad.
Help out your big sister, or brother
so small. Because PEOPLE are
the greatest miracle of all!